IT'S OKAY TO BE THE BOSS

THE MANAGEMENT WORKSHOP

PARTICIPANT WORKBOOK

BRUCE TULGAN

A Wiley Imprint
www.pfeiffer.com

ISBN: 978-0-470-40534-5

Acquiring Editor: Lisa Shannon
Developmental Editor: Janis Fisher Chan
Editor: Rebecca Taff
Composition: Leigh McLellan Design
Printed in the United States of America

Director of Development: Kathleen Dolan Davies
Production Editor: Dawn Kilgore
Manufacturing Supervisor: Becky Morgan
Design: Gearbox

Printing 10 9 8 7 6 5 4

CONTENTS

WHAT'S HARD ABOUT MANAGING?

What do you find most challenging about managing people?

_____

_____

_____

_____

_____

_____

_____

_____

_____

_____

_____

_____

_____

_____

_____

_____

_____

_____

_____

"If you manage people, you already have management habits that feel right— good habits feel right, and bad habits feel right. The goal today is to figure out whether there is room to improve."

YOUR OBJECTIVES

What would you like to accomplish in this workshop?

_____

_____

_____

_____

_____

_____

_____

_____

_____

_____

_____

_____

_____

_____

_____

_____

_____

WORKSHOP OBJECTIVES

WHAT DO YOU WANT TO ACCOMPLISH?

WHEN YOU COMPLETE THIS WORKSHOP, YOU WILL BE ABLE TO:

- Explain the importance to yourself, your employees, and your organization of being a strong, highly engaged manager

- Describe common obstacles to being an engaged manager, explain which obstacles you can control and how to control them, and describe strategies for working around obstacles you cannot control

- Describe eight back-to-basics techniques for helping your employees succeed

- Develop an action plan for applying the eight techniques to improve your ability to be a great boss

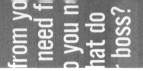

THE BASICS OF MANAGING PEOPLE

What do you need from your boss? What can your boss do to help you succeed at your job?

_____

_____

_____

_____

_____

_____

_____

_____

_____

_____

_____

_____

_____

_____

_____

_____

THE CONSEQUENCES OF UNDER-MANAGEMENT

- *Fires start that should never have started.*

- *Fires get out of control that could have been put out easily.*

- *Resources are squandered.*

- *People go in the wrong direction for days, weeks, and months on end before anyone notices.*

- *Low performers hide out and collect their paychecks.*

- *Mediocre performers convince themselves that they are the high performers.*

- *High performers become frustrated and think about leaving.*

- *Leaders and managers do tasks that should have been delegated to someone else—or they may be delegated to someone else, and then delegated back up to you.*

- *Other:*

FIGHT THE UNDER-MANAGEMENT EPIDEMIC: BE A GREAT BOSS!

You don't need permission to . . .

1. Get in the habit of managing every day.

2. Learn to talk like a performance coach.

3. Take it one person at a time.

4. Make accountability a real process, not a slogan.

5. Make expectations clear; tell people what to do and how to do it.

6. Track performance in writing every step of the way.

7. Solve small problems before they turn into big ones.

8. Do more for some people and less for others.

REAL-WORLD OBSTACLES

What real-world obstacles make it hard for you to be a strong, highly engaged manager?

_____

_____

_____

_____

_____

_____

_____

_____

_____

_____

_____

_____

_____

_____

_____

_____

THE TOP SEVEN MANAGEMENT MYTHS

MYTH 1: EMPOWERMENT _____

_____

_____

MYTH 2: FAIRNESS _____

_____

_____

MYTH 3: JERK BOSS _____

_____

_____

MYTH 4: CONFRONTATION _____

_____

_____

MYTH 5: RED TAPE _____

_____

_____

MYTH 6: NATURAL LEADER _____

_____

_____

MYTH 7: TIME _____

_____

_____

NOTES

BACK-TO-BASICS TECHNIQUE 1

GET IN THE HABIT OF MANAGING EVERY DAY

Managers who are positively convinced that they don't have any time, spend more time managing them anyone else. They just spend all their management time in crisis mode. If you don't spend time managing up-front, in advance, before anything goes wrong, you will spend all of your management time solving problems that never should have happened in the first place and doing work that other people should be doing.

You don't have time *not* to manage.

_____

_____

_____

_____

_____

_____

_____

_____

_____

_____

_____

_____

_____

_____

ONE-ON-ONE CONVERSATIONS WITH THE PEOPLE YOU MANAGE

Focus on the work—
expectations, goals, deadlines,
problems.

_____

_____

_____

Ask for concrete details about
how things are going

_____

_____

_____

Talk through the work that
needs to be done. Ask, "What
steps are you going to follow?"

_____

_____

_____

Tell them how to avoid
unnecessary pitfalls.

_____

_____

_____

Tell employees what you need
from them.

_____

_____

_____

Ask what they need from you.

_____

_____

_____

GETTING STARTED

Focus on three to five people a day.

_____

_____

_____

Keep the meetings short, no more than fifteen minutes.

_____

_____

_____

Consider having stand-up meetings, with a clipboard in hand for taking notes.

_____

_____

_____

Meet with everyone at least once every two weeks.

_____

_____

_____

If any of your employees work on other shifts, stay late or come in early to meet with them.

_____

_____

_____

If you manage people in different locations, use phone and e-mail regularly when you can't have one-on-one meetings.

_____

_____

_____

HOW TO MAKE TIME AVAILABLE

Make a commitment and stick
with it.

_____

_____

_____

Block out the time on your schedule.

_____

_____

_____

Try different schedules, different
days and times, and see what
works best.

_____

_____

_____

Make appointments with each
individual for each one-on-one and
keep them.

_____

_____

_____

Endow the time for one-on-ones
with the same characteristics as
other things you do routinely.

_____

_____

_____

Figure out what information can
be communicated at brief team
meetings and set up some one-on-
ones after those meetings.

_____

_____

_____

WORKSHEET: MAKING TIME FOR MANAGING EVERY DAY

1. What will you do to make the time available for regular one-on-one meetings with the people you manage?

   •

   •

   •

   •

2. Look at your schedule for the next four weeks and block out an hour a day for one-on-one conversations with your employees.

Sunday	Monday	Tuesday	Wednesday	Thursday	Friday	Saturday
1	2	3	4	5	6	7
8	9	10	11	12	13	14
15	16	17	18	19	20	21
22	23	24	25	26	27	28
29	30	31				

BACK-TO-BASICS TECHNIQUE 2

LEARN TO TALK LIKE A PERFORMANCE COACH

The best performance coaches talk like teachers—people who care enough about the other person's success to spend time guiding and directing. They have lots of one-on-one conversations with direct reports about the work, and they break things down, using specific, concrete language that spells things out.

A coach . . .

- *Tells people what they are supposed to do and how to do it*

- *Helps people build their skills*

- *Monitors performance and gives feedback*

- *Provides encouragement and support*

- *Helps people solve problems*

NOTES

HOW A COACH TALKS

NOT THIS (NAMING)	**BUT THIS (DESCRIPTION)**
You're working too slowly.	It was due Tuesday at 2:00 and you turned it in Thursday at 3:00.
Your work is too sloppy.	You made serious mistakes in three of the last five orders you processed.
You've got a bad attitude.	You're walking around this place with a grimace on your face and you keep growling at people.
Your work is very professional.	Your last three reports were well written, polished, and turned in on time.

_____

_____

_____

_____

_____

_____

_____

_____

_____

_____

_____

DISCUSSION QUESTIONS FOR COACHING CONVERSATIONS

How should you approach this person?

_____

_____

_____

What is your goal?

_____

_____

_____

What is your message?

_____

_____

_____

How will you begin the conversation?

_____

_____

_____

How will you get the information on the table?

_____

_____

_____

What points do you need to make?

_____

_____

_____

_____

What broad performance standards do you want to reinforce?

_____

_____

_____

_____

What concrete next steps do you want to suggest/require?

_____

_____

_____

_____

What kind of follow-up conversation will you schedule? When? Where?

_____

_____

_____

_____

COACHING SCRIPT

Make a script with bullet points for what you want to say during the coaching conversation.

1. **The beginning:** What will you say to get the conversation started?

_____

_____

_____

_____

2. **The information:** What will you say to get the information on the table?

_____

_____

_____

_____

3. **The direction:** What will you say to give the person concrete next steps?

_____

_____

_____

_____

4. **The timing:** When will you have this conversation?

_____

_____

_____

QUESTIONS TO ASK DURING A COACHING CONVERSATION

What did you do?

_____

_____

_____

How did you do it?

_____

_____

_____

What are you going to do next?

_____

_____

_____

How are you going to do it?

_____

_____

_____

What steps are you going to follow?

_____

_____

_____

What step are you on now?

_____

_____

How long is that going to take?

_____

_____

_____

FOR USEFUL COACHING CONVERSATIONS

Step One: Prepare for the conversation in writing.

Step Two: Conduct the conversation. Describe performance, break it down, and spell it out. "Here's what I know. Tell me what I don't know. Here's what I want you to do next." Set goals and deadlines.

Step Three: Follow up, follow up, follow up.

_____

_____

_____

_____

_____

_____

_____

_____

_____

_____

_____

_____

_____

WORKSHEET: COACHING SCRIPT

Make a script with bullet points for what you want to say during the coaching conversation.

Name (or Code Name): _____

When you will have this conversation: _____

1. **The beginning:** What will you say to get the conversation started?

   _____

   _____

   _____

2. **The information:** What will you say to get the information on the table?

   _____

   _____

   _____

3. **The direction:** What will you say to give the person concrete next steps?

   _____

   _____

   _____

4. **The timing:** When will you have this conversation?

   _____

   _____

   _____

BACK-TO-BASICS TECHNIQUE 3

TAKE IT ONE PERSON AT A TIME

In what ways do the people you manage differ from one another? What makes it easier for you to manage one, and more challenging to manage another?

-

-

-

-

-

-

-

SIX QUESTIONS FOR TUNING IN TO EACH PERSON YOU MANAGE:

WHO is this person *at work*?

High performer, low performer, or somewhere in the middle?

High productivity, low productivity, or somewhere in the middle?

High-quality work, low-quality work, or somewhere in the middle?

Irritating behaviors that you want him or her to stop? Positive behaviors you want others to emulate?

_____

_____

_____

WHY do you need to manage this person?

What is your goal with this person? Work faster or slower? Improve quality? Stop dotting the i's and get on with it? Adopt a new behavior?

_____

_____

_____

_____

WHAT should you be saying to this person during a one-on-one?

What do you want the person to focus on between now and the next time you talk?

_____

_____

_____

_____

HOW should you talk to this person?

Direct questions? Indirect questions? Send an e-mail first?

_____

_____

_____

_____

_____

WHERE should you talk to this person?

At the person's desk? At your desk? In a stairwell? In the cafeteria?

_____

_____

_____

_____

_____

WHEN should you talk to this person?

On his or her way in the door? Out the door? During the day?

How often should you talk to the person? How much guidance and direction does the person need?

_____

_____

_____

_____

TUNING-IN TOOL

Answer these questions about one of the people you manage.

Name (or Code Name): _____

WHO is this person *at work*?

_____

_____

WHY do you need to manage this person? What is your goal with this person?

_____

_____

WHAT should you be saying to this person during a one-on-one?

_____

_____

HOW should you talk to this person?

_____

_____

WHERE should you talk to this person?

_____

_____

WHEN should you talk to this person? How often?

_____

_____

WHEN

WHERE

HOW

WHAT

WHY

WHO

WORKSHEET: MANAGER'S LANDSCAPE

BACK-TO-BASICS TECHNIQUE 4

MAKE ACCOUNTABILITY A PROCESS, NOT A SLOGAN

Accountability means:

- *Having to explain your actions to another person.*

- *Understanding that actions have consequences.*

_____

_____

_____

_____

To hold people accountable:

- *Tell then what you want them to do—spell it out.*

- *Monitor their performance closely and accurately and write things down.*

- *Make sure there are real consequences to meeting or not meeting the expectations.*

_____

_____

_____

_____

_____

TOP SEVEN COMPLICATIONS TO ACCOUNTABILITY

"I'm waiting for so-and-so or such-and-such."

_____

_____

_____

"Some other work obligations got in the way."

_____

_____

_____

You've been accepting mediocrity for a long time.

_____

_____

_____

You're a brand-new manager or new to the team.

_____

_____

_____

Some of the people you are managing are your friends.

_____

_____

_____

You don't have direct authority over someone you manage.

_____

_____

_____

You manage people doing work in areas in which you don't have knowledge or experience.

_____

_____

KEY ACTIONS FOR HOLDING PEOPLE ACCOUNTABLE

Get them in the habit of explaining
their actions.

_____

_____

_____

Spell out what they are expected to
do and make sure they have the
resources to do it.

_____

_____

_____

Make sure that people know there
will be real consequences to their
performance.

_____

_____

_____

Keep the focus on concrete actions
that the person can control.

_____

_____

_____

Monitor the person's performance
fairly and accurately.

_____

_____

_____

Put things in writing.

_____

_____

Separate your role as a friend from
your role as the boss.

_____

_____

If you don't have direct authority,
use influence and persuasion.

_____

WORKSHEET: STRATEGIES FOR HOLDING PEOPLE ACCOUNTABLE

What strategies will you use to hold someone you manage accountable?

Name (or Code Name): _____

Strategies:

_____

_____

_____

_____

_____

_____

_____

_____

_____

_____

_____

_____

_____

BACK-TO-BASICS TECHNIQUE 5

MAKE EXPECTATIONS CLEAR EVERY STEP OF THE WAY

1. Think of someone you manage who is about to start a new task, is having trouble with a process or procedure, has a performance problem, or needs to improve some element of his or her performance.

   Name (or Code Name): _____

2. Describe exactly what you want the person to do.

   _____

   _____

   _____

   _____

   _____

   _____

3. Read the description to a partner and ask for feedback: "If you were this person, what would be clear, and what would not be clear? What other information would you need?"

4. Use the space below to revise the description so it clearly spells out what you want the person to do.

   _____

   _____

   _____

   _____

MAKE EXPECTATIONS CLEAR EVERY STEP OF THE WAY

Managers commonly complain that they shouldn't have to tell people how to do things. But the same managers complain that too many people fail to meet their expectations. Telling people what to do and telling them how to do it is the essence of real accountability and setting people up for success.

> # Tell people what to do and how to do it— the essence of real accountability and setting people up for success.

TURN BEST PRACTICES INTO CHECKLISTS

Checklists make things go better. If you want to make sure your one-on-ones are about guiding and directing someone in the work he or she is doing, the last step in the conversation is to go over what you've agreed on and make a checklist. Say to the person, "Tell me what you're going to do. Tell me how you're going to get started. Tell me what steps you're going to follow." Then help the person make a checklist: "Let's write down what we've agreed about what you are going to do between now and the next time we meet."

NOTES

TO DELEGATE SUCCESSFULLY

Make the expectation clear;
give person a clear goal, a time-
line, guidelines, and parameters.

_____

_____

_____

_____

_____

_____

Help the person make a plan;
use a checklist.

_____

_____

_____

_____

_____

_____

Meet with the person one-on-one
as often as needed. Did the person
accomplish everything on the
checklist? If not, why not? Is there
something the person needs
from you?

_____

_____

_____

_____

_____

_____

CIRCLES OF EMPOWERMENT

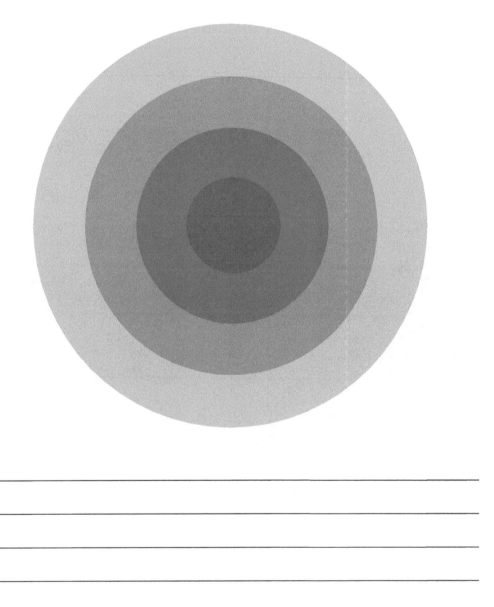

_____

_____

_____

_____

_____

_____

_____

BACK-TO-BASICS TECHNIQUE 6

TRACK PERFORMANCE IN WRITING

If you're going to be able to talk to people about their performance, you need to monitor that performance. Here are five ways to do that:

1. Watch people work.

2. Check their work in progress.

3. Give them self-monitoring tools (the checklist).

4. Get information from others.

5. Ask the person for an account on a regular basis.

TO EVALUATE PERFORMANCE

The only fair way to evaluate a person's performance is to compare that performance against the checklist and ask these questions:

- *Did the person achieve the goals you had established in advance?*

- *Did he or she do the tasks, and do them the way they were supposed to be done?*

- *Did he or she meet the deadlines you had agreed on?*

NOTES

REASONS FOR WRITING THINGS DOWN

- *It's easy to lose track unless you write things down.*

- *Keeping track in writing sends a powerful message that you are taking this very seriously.*

- *A written record trumps differing recollections.*

- *If you need help from HR, they need written documentation.*

NOTES

SYSTEMS FOR TRACKING PERFORMANCE IN WRITING

You need a system for documenting performance that works for you, that is easy for you, that you know you can stick with. What are some systems you could use to track performance in writing?

-

-

-

-

-

-

-

DESCRIBE, DESCRIBE, DESCRIBE

Never name behavior or write down assumptions about a person's motivations or thoughts. Instead, describe . . .

- *The expectations and what the employee will do to meet those expectations.*

- *The employee's actual performance—what you observe, what the employee says, the observable results of the employee's work, and what other people say about the employee's work.*

NOTES

WORKSHEET: TRACKING PERFORMANCE IN WRITING

Select one employee and do the following:

1. Write the person's name (or code name):

2. Think of some performance you observed recently. Describe the expectation:

_____

_____

_____

_____

_____

3. Describe your observations of the person's concrete actions and how they measured up to the expectations:

_____

_____

_____

_____

_____

NOTES:

_____

_____

_____

_____

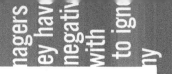

BACK-TO-BASICS TECHNIQUE 7

SOLVE SMALL PROBLEMS EARLY BEFORE THEY TURN INTO BIG ONES

Because they dislike giving negative feedback, too many managers put off dealing directly with performance problems until they have grown too large to ignore. The best way to keep small problems from becoming huge ones is to be a strong, highly engaged manager who spends time one-on-one with each person, talks to the person directly and candidly, customizes an approach to managing that person, makes expectations clear, and tracks performance every step of the way.

Instead of having to confront massive problems once in a while, deal with one small problem at a time in the course of your regular one-on-one conversations. Instead of meeting with the employee under stress to confront a problem that you both know has been going on for a while, let the employee know that you are paying close attention so that you can help him or her be successful.

DIAGNOSING PERFORMANCE PROBLEMS

Ability: Are the person's natural strengths a poor match for the job?

_____

_____

_____

_____

Skill: Does the employee lack knowledge, information, skills, tools, or other resources to do the job?

_____

_____

_____

_____

Will: Is the employee motivated to do the job?

_____

_____

_____

_____

WORKSHEET: DIAGNOSING A PERSISTENT PERFORMANCE PROBLEM

Describe a persistent performance problem with a current employee.

Name (or Code Name): _____

1. What is the problem?

   _____

   _____

   _____

   _____

2. How long has the problem been going on?

   _____

   _____

   _____

   _____

3. Use the Ability/Skill/Will model to diagnose the problem. Into which category does this problem appear to fall?

   ☐ **Ability**   ☐ **Skill**   ☐ **Will**

4. Describe any efforts you have made to help the employee solve the problem:

   _____

   _____

   _____

   _____

5. Write a script for talking to the employee about the problem that includes the concrete actions you want the person to take:

- How will you get the conversation started?

  _____

  _____

  _____

- How will you get the information on the table?

  _____

  _____

  _____

- What concrete next steps will you give the person?

  _____

  _____

  _____

"Managers have an obligation to be strong and highly engaged, hands-on and transactional—to help people earn what they want and what they need, and to set them up for success."

BACK-TO-BASICS TECHNIQUE 8

DO MORE FOR SOME PEOPLE, LESS FOR OTHERS

Being fair does not mean treating everyone the same because:

- *People perform differently.*

- *People need different things from you.*

- *High-performing employees are worth more than low-performing employees.*

- *High-performing employees deserve more than low-performing employees.*

Give all employees the chance to meet the basic expectations of their jobs and then the chance to go above and beyond—and to be rewarded accordingly. When your employees deliver on their commitments for you, you deliver on promised rewards for them. If they fail to meet commitments, call them on that failure immediately and withhold the reward.

EXAMPLES OF WHAT MANAGERS DO TO TREAT EVERYONE FAIRLY:

_____

_____

_____

_____

_____

_____

_____

THREE TRENDS IN REWARDS

Control: Ask people to tell you what they want and then tell them how to earn it.

_____

_____

_____

_____

_____

Timing: Rewards are more effective when they are given in close proximity to an event.

_____

_____

_____

_____

_____

Customization: Except for money, people want different things, so customize rewards for each individual.

_____

_____

_____

_____

_____

What are some non-monetary rewards people care about that you can control?

_____

_____

_____

_____

USING REWARDS AS INCENTIVES AND QUID PRO QUOS

What are some ways in which you can use rewards to drive performance and retain valuable employees?

_____

_____

_____

_____

_____

_____

_____

_____

_____

_____

_____

_____

_____

_____

_____

_____

WORKSHEET: "WHAT CAN YOU DO TO EARN THAT?"

Person's Name (or Code Name):

1. Describe this person's performance:

    ☐ A high performer   ☐ A low performer   ☐ Somewhere in-between

2. What does this person care about that you can control?

    ☐ **Schedule:** Change in working hours? Flexible hours? Four-day work week?
    Other?

    _____

    ☐ **Relationships:** Which colleagues, customers, vendors, and others would the
    person like or prefer not to work with?

    _____

    ☐ **Tasks:** What tasks and responsibilities would the employee like or not like to
    work on?

    _____

    ☐ **Learning opportunities:** Are there special learning opportunities the employee
    would like to have?

    _____

    ☐ **Location:** Where would the employee like to work? Degree of control the person
    would like to have over the workspace? Opportunities to travel or not to travel?

    _____

    ☐ **Other:**

    _____

3. What could the person do to earn what he or she wants or needs?

_____

_____

_____

_____

4. Write a script for talking with the person:

- How will you get the conversation started?

  _____

  _____

  _____

  _____

- How will you get the information on the table?

  _____

  _____

  _____

  _____

- What concrete next steps will you give the person?

  _____

  _____

  _____

  _____

WORKSHEET: "WHAT CAN YOU DO TO EARN THAT?"

Person's Name (or Code Name):

1. Describe this person's performance:

   ☐ A high performer   ☐ A low performer   ☐ Somewhere in-between

2. What does this person care about that you can control?

   ☐ **Schedule:** Change in working hours? Flexible hours? Four-day work week? Other?

   _____

   ☐ **Relationships:** Which colleagues, customers, vendors, and others would the person like or prefer not to work with?

   _____

   ☐ **Tasks:** What tasks and responsibilities would the employee like or not like to work on?

   _____

   ☐ **Learning opportunities:** Are there special learning opportunities the employee would like to have?

   _____

   ☐ **Location:** Where would the employee like to work? Degree of control the person would like to have over the workspace? Opportunities to travel or not to travel?

   _____

   ☐ **Other:**

   _____

3. What could the person do to earn what he or she wants or needs?

_____

_____

_____

_____

4. Write a script for talking with the person:

- How will you get the conversation started?

_____

_____

_____

_____

- How will you get the information on the table?

_____

_____

_____

_____

- What concrete next steps will you give the person?

_____

_____

_____

_____

MANAGER'S CHECKLIST

☐ Set aside one hour a day to manage your employees, and—at first—use that time to prepare.

☐ As you talk with your employees about the work, practice talking like a performance coach.

☐ Create your manager's landscape. Lay out the six key questions at the top of a piece of paper and answer them about each employee: Who, Why, What, How, Where, and When.

☐ Make a preliminary schedule for coaching.

☐ Create your own tracking system.

☐ Reach out to key people [such as your boss and others who manage this person] and discuss your coaching plans.

☐ Start a regular schedule of ongoing one-on-one coaching conversations.

☐ Stay flexible. Revise and adjust every step of the way.

ACTIONS FOR BECOMING A BETTER BOSS

_____

_____

_____

_____

_____

_____

_____

_____

_____

_____

_____

_____

_____

_____

_____

_____

_____

_____

_____

_____

_____

WORKSHEET: ACTION PLANNING

What concrete actions can you take to apply what you have learned in this workshop?

ACTIONS   **DEADLINE**

_____   _____

_____   _____

_____   _____

_____   _____

_____   _____

_____   _____

_____   _____

_____   _____

_____   _____

_____   _____

_____   _____

_____   _____

_____   _____

_____   _____

_____   _____

_____   _____

APPENDIX

COACHING SCRIPT

TUNING-IN TOOL

MANAGER'S LANDSCAPE

"WHAT CAN YOU DO TO EARN THAT?"

COACHING SCRIPT

Make a script with bullet points for what you want to say during the coaching conversation.

Name (or Code Name):

When you will have this conversation:

1. The beginning: What will you say to get the conversation started?

_____

_____

_____

2. The information: What will you say to get the information on the table?

_____

_____

_____

3. The direction: What will you say to give the person concrete next steps?

_____

_____

_____

4. The timing: When will you have this conversation?

_____

_____

_____

TUNING-IN TOOL

Name (or Code Name):

WHO is this person at work?

_____

_____

WHY do you need to manage this person? What is your goal with this person?

_____

_____

WHAT should you be saying to this person during a one-on-one?

_____

_____

HOW should you talk to this person?

_____

_____

WHERE should you talk to this person?

_____

_____

WHEN should you talk to this person? How often?

_____

_____

WORKSHEET: MANAGER'S LANDSCAPE

WHO	WHY	WHAT	HOW	WHERE	WHEN

"WHAT CAN YOU DO TO EARN THAT?"

Person's Name (or Code Name):

1. Describe this person's performance:

   ☐ A high performer   ☐ A low performer   ☐ Somewhere in-between

2. What does this person care about that you can control?

   ☐ **Schedule:** Change in working hours? Flexible hours? Four-day work week? Other?

   _____

   ☐ **Relationships:** Which colleagues, customers, vendors, and others would the person like or prefer not to work with?

   _____

   ☐ **Tasks:** What tasks and responsibilities would the employee like or not like to work on?

   _____

   ☐ **Learning opportunities:** Are there special learning opportunities the employee would like to have?

   _____

   ☐ **Location:** Where would the employee like to work? Degree of control the person would like to have over the workspace? Opportunities to travel or not to travel?

   _____

   ☐ **Other:**

   _____

3. What could the person do to earn what he or she wants or needs?

_____

_____

_____

_____

4. Write a script for talking with the person:

- How will you get the conversation started?

_____

_____

_____

_____

- How will you get the information on the table?

_____

_____

_____

_____

- What concrete next steps will you give the person?

_____

_____

_____

_____

ABOUT THE AUTHOR

BRUCE TULGAN (New Haven, CT) is internationally recognized as a leading expert on leadership and management. He is an advisor to business leaders all over the world, the author or coauthor of numerous books, most recently *Not Everyone Gets a Trophy: How to Manage Generation Y* (Jossey-Bass, 2009), the classic *Managing Generation X* (1995), and the recent best-seller *It's Okay to Be the Boss* (2007). Since founding the management training firm RainmakerThinking in 1993, he has been a sought-after keynote speaker and seminar leader. Tulgan has personally trained tens of thousands of managers in a wide range of industries. His work has been the subject of thousands of news stories around the world, and he has written for dozens of publications, including *The New York Times*, *USA Today*, *Human Resources* magazine, and *The Harvard Business Review*. He also holds a fourth degree black belt in Okinawan Karate and is married to Debby Applegate, who won the 2007 Pulitzer Prize for Biography. Tulgan's weekly v-log (video newsletter) is available for free at www.rainmakerthinking.com.

What will you find on pfeiffer.com?

- The best in workplace performance solutions for training and HR professionals
- Downloadable training tools, exercises, and content
- Web-exclusive offers
- Training tips, articles, and news
- Seamless on-line ordering
- Author guidelines, information on becoming a Pfeiffer Affiliate, and much more

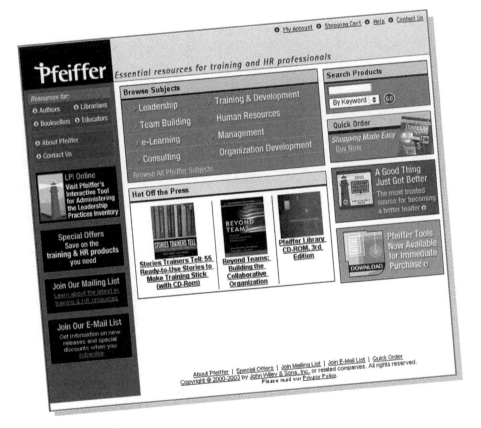

Discover more at www.pfeiffer.com